CYBERAMA

By Arthi Vasudevan

CyberSecYOUrity! Thanks for doing your part in keeping the world cyber safe!

- ARTHI

ISBN 13: 978-1-63489-634-4

Library of Congress Catalog Number has been applied for.
Printed in the United States of America
First Printing: 2023
27   26   25   24   23   5   4   3   2   1

Illustrations by Jasmin Davis
Design by Vivian Steckline
Content strategy and project management by Victoria Petelin
Concept review by Anish Rangan and Archana Vasudevan
Developmental editing by Lee Nordling
Copy editing by Stephanie Bize

Wise Ink Creative Publishing
807 Broadway St. NE, Suite 46
Minneapolis, MN 55413
wiseink.com

To order, visit itascabooks.com, cyberama.org, or call 1-800-901-3480. Reseller discounts available.

Disclaimer: All characters and events in this publication of Cyberama are fictitious and any resemblance to real persons, living or dead, is purely coincidental. The book does not constitute actionable advice, and is meant to serve as a learning guide on digital safety and cybersecurity. The idea and story are original, and the contents provided in this book are for educational purposes. No liability is assumed for losses or damages due to the information provided.

For my nephew Anish,
who inspired me and stayed with me
throughout the writing of this book,
and my kids Aadhav and Adithi

FOREWORD

Our world is full of technology, count how many devices you plug or unplug each day. Technology creates new and imaginary places, and helps us stay connected with people. Our senses are constantly ignited by technology as it shapes and vividly colors our world. Technology also helps us increase our wisdom, and provides easy access to education for those who otherwise cannot afford it.

However, excessive use of technology through devices can have negative side effects on people of all ages. In this digital age, as we are connected to strangers via technology, it is also important to understand what level of exposure and digital trail we leave behind on the internet. In *Cyberama*, you will explore how to be safe and healthy while using technology. The author has used physical security as an analogy to explain digital cybersecurity. Be sure to bag some pretty neat cybersecurity words too, new words you can actually use daily while chatting with your pals or family!

The power of technology can guide our world, but let's not let it define us.

—Erin Twamley
Award-winning Children's Book Author, STEM Educator,
Clean Energy Champion and Eduprenuer

PLAY THE
"CYBERAMA GAME"
ALONGSIDE THE BOOK'S CHARACTERS, MAYA AND DAVE!

Want more fun? Play the online Cyberama game with your own avatar and learn how to beat Cyber Ninjas in real life!

With six fast-paced levels of game play, players must venture inside the human body, into a castle, and even through the Metaverse to defeat the hackers. . . before it's too late.

Will you capture all the flags when your cybersecurity knowledge is put to the test?

Log onto **cyberama.org** with a parent or guardian to play the FREE computer game.

MEET THE
CHARACTERS

NAME	MAYA
PLAYER ID	MYSTERIOUS MAYA
SKILL	CURIOSITY
FAV FOOD	CHEESE SANDWICH
MISSION	STAY OUT OF TROUBLE

NAME	DAVE
PLAYER ID	DYNAMITE DAVE
SKILL	VIDEO GAMING
FAV FOOD	PIZZA
MISSION	PLAY CYBERAMA

NAME	MAYA'S PARENTS
SKILL	RESEARCH
FAV FOOD	SOUP
MISSION	PROJECT X

NAME	CYBER OWL
PLAYER ID	WISE OLE OWL
SKILL	SUPERSONIC SPEED
FAV FOOD	CYBER MOTH
MISSION	HELP MAYA

NAME	CYBER PANDA
PLAYER ID	PERKY PANDA
SKILL	TRACKING IP ADDRESS
FAV FOOD	BAMBOO
MISSION	HELP MAYA

NAME	CYBER ELLA
PLAYER ID	ELEGANT ELLA
SKILL	FLAME THROWER
FAV FOOD	CANDY CORN
MISSION	HELP MAYA

NAME	CYBER MEOW
PLAYER ID	MAJESTIC MEOW
SKILL	SURPRISE
FAV FOOD	RASPBERRY PIE
MISSION	HELP MAYA

NAME	CYBER FOX
PLAYER ID	FURIOUS FOX
SKILL	WIT
FAV FOOD	CYBERBITS
MISSION	HELP MAYA

NAME	CYBER KIKI
PLAYER ID	FLAMINGO FANTASTIC
SKILL	LASER BEAM
FAV FOOD	SHRIMP
MISSION	HELP MAYA

NAME	CYBERCRIMINALS
SKILL	HACKING
FAV FOOD	RANDOM STUFF
MISSION	TOP SECRET

CONTENTS

1

THE GAME

I would have laughed really hard and said, "No way!" if you had told me that I, a twelve-year-old Indian American New Yorker named Maya Iyer, would go places like a parallel universe, a magical rainforest, and inside the human body. If you said that this girl, who feels lost most of the time and is trying to figure out who she really is, would fight dangerous cybercriminals, along with crazy, wacky, *artificially intelligent (AI)* animal creatures to save the world, I wouldn't have believed you. But yeah, all of that happened, and much, much more.

So let me take you to that time when these crazy adventures happened. Let's actually go there, so you feel like it's happening right now.

• • •

"Mayaaaaa!" shouts Dave, my best friend and neighbor, as he comes running with his twenty-pound, navy blue galaxy school bag, which looks bigger than him. He isn't the only kid in Scarsdale, New York who carries a heavy backpack.

"Hi Dave, I was just going to come by. I have to tell you something."

"And, I have to tell you something… But you go first," replies Dave.

"Guess what my parents got me for my birthday?"

"A new video-game console? A new bike? A trip to Magic Wonderland?" he asks.

"Nope, close! They got me my own personal tablet! A brand-new, shiny, silver tablet with lots of apps and some games!"

"Whoa! This is cool, and the timing couldn't be any better!"

"Why is that?" I ask. Dave seems excited. His blue eyes become bigger and wider.

"So, there is a new *virtual reality (VR)* game

called *Cyberama* that everyone is playing. I mean EVERYONE—kids in my class, your class, everyone at our school, and probably other schools. We've got to play this game, like TODAY!"

"Really? I haven't heard of it. What kind of a VR game is that?" I ask.

"I haven't played the game either, but I'm hearing great things about it. I promise it's going to be AWWWESOME! I'm going to go home and get changed. Let's meet at your house in an hour, okay? See ya!" Dave disappears before I wave him bye. I haven't seen him this excited since he got picked for the basketball team last year. Then again, he gets like this every time he stuffs his mouth with over thirty fries! We actually counted once. He can fit thirty-six and a half fries into his mouth, to be exact.

I come home, excited to tell my parents about playing the game *Cyberama*. They've been swamped lately with some kind of science project they've been working on for months. They've always been hardworking scientists. I'm not sure if they want me to be a scientist when I grow up—I could be. I like computers.

KNOCK, KNOCK.

"Mom! Dad! I'm home!" I call as I knock at their door. The door cracks open, and through it, I can see books piled up, two microscopes, and some lab specimen my parents keep looking at all day. Mom steps out of the room, and as Dad's wheelchair rolls out, he quickly closes the door behind them.

"What's going on, Maya? You seem excited!" Mom says.

"Mom! Dad! Guess what? Dave said he wants to play a VR game with me. I'm super excited!"

"That's cool! "What kind of VR game? Did your school recommend it?" asks Dad. Dad always teaches me cool computer tricks, like keyboard shortcuts and how to minimize tens of windows at once.

"Dave told me. He said everyone in my class and our school is playing it. I definitely want to check it out!" I reply.

"Hmm, okay," Dad says. He then turns to mom.

"Tara, I think it's time to introduce Maya's new friends to her." Mom nods her head. Dad opens the door behind him, goes to the closet, and brings along six mini animal robots. I hear the whirring sound of the bots, puzzled about what they are.

"Maya, listen. Since you'll be connected to the internet to learn new things, and now that you are playing VR games, we want to make sure you make safe digital choices. Your dad and I designed these mini, artificially-intelligent robots, or AI bots—your cyber pals—to help you stay safe in the digital space," Mom explains.

"But Mom, Dad, don't you think I'm grown enough to take care of myself?"

"You sure are, princess! But you can never be too digitally safe! The internet can be a scary place, filled with both good and bad people. Your cyber pals will help you as you navigate your way on the internet."

Mom introduces them one by one. "Meet Cyber Kiki!" She motions at a pinkish, translucent flamingo wearing VR goggles, who seems to struggle to stand on its two legs.

"Here's Cyber Fox!" She turns me toward a silly-looking orange fox with funky eyes.

"This is Cyber Ella!" A stark white comical unicorn

with a rainbow-colored mane and tail, wearing sunglasses, faces me.

"I would like to introduce you to Cyber Owl!" A brown owl looks at me suspiciously. He has hypnotizing green and black eyes, a white hat, and a super weird old-guy beard.

"Meet Cyber Panda!" An innocent-looking panda, who, I'm sure doesn't know any cool tricks from Kung Fu or Jujitsu, looks at me up and down.

"And last but not least, Cyber Meow!" A black

cat with green eyes, super-cute eyelashes, and a gray hoodie stands there. She actually looks like a computer **hacker**—one that steals people's information for money.

Mom then turns around to the animal bots and says, "Cyber pals, meet Maya!"

Umm, these folks are my cyber pals and will protect me? Is this a joke? A comic palooza my parents want me to be a part of? As I look at my new bot pals, many thoughts run through my mind.

"Maya," Dad says, "We invented these computer bots because these were some of your favorite animals when you were little. Here, look at the handle of my chair."

I look at the right handle of Dad's wheelchair and see worn-out stickers of a flamingo, owl, panda, fox, cat, and a unicorn.

"These bots have feelings, too," he continues. "They also have special powers to control computers. Just wait and see."

AI animal bots with feelings who will watch me all the time and can unleash **supercomputer powers**? Why couldn't my parents have just gotten me a smartphone instead? Everyone in my class has a smartphone, and they text *all the time*! Some are even on social media without their parents knowing it! And here I am, hanging out with robots that my parents designed to be my watchdogs! No wonder my classmate Elise thinks I'm a nerd!

I turn to my new pals and say, "Hey folks, it's nice to meet you. . . I guess?"

"Now, if you'll excuse us, your mom and I have to get back to research," Dad says.

"C'mon Dad, you both do research all day. Why don't we spend some time playing a card game?" I ask.

"Ah, Maya… We are working on a project with a very tight deadline," he replies.

"Dad, what's the project about? Can I see? Pleeeeeease."

"We'd love to show you honey—but we can't. It's a research project for the government, and we aren't allowed to talk about it, even to family. Let's call it Project X, and it can save millions of lives. We'll meet you for dinner, okay? Grilled cheese sandwiches, your favorite. Your pals will keep you company until then," he says, kissing me on my forehead.

"Okay… Bye Dad, bye Mom. I guess I'll see you soon." I turn to the pals, but I hear someone at the door before I can say anything.

KNOCK! KNOCK!

I rush to the front door. It's Dave. I introduce Dave to my new cyber pals, and Dave's excitement instantly doubles! We've always been the nerdy kids at school, the ones who like to fiddle with computers, and now I guess—robots. After examining the bots from top to bottom and learning their names, Dave looks at me and says, "Your cyber pals are *super cool*! Hey, is there a Cyber Dino by any chance? Or a Cyber Bear?"

"You wish! These bots were designed after my favorite animals as a child, not yours," I laugh.

Dave laughs, too, before opening his tablet and handing me a pair of VR glasses.

"C'mon, Maya, are you ready? Let's play!"

When I open my tablet, a dialog box asks me to set a password.

"Oh yeah, I have to set a password. I've been ignoring it since I got the tablet."

"Do it later, Maya. Hurry! Let's play the game. I can't wait!" Dave exclaims.

"Okay, I guess I'll do it later."

We enter the website address and download the game.

As we're about to enter the game, and start playing as players one and two, Cyber Kiki asks, "Hey, you two! Can I join as player three, just to watch the game?"

"I guess it can't hurt," I say.

Dave and I put on our VR goggles. Cyber Kiki already wears a set.

"Wow, this feels so real!" I exclaim as I feel like I'm in the middle of a deep blue ocean. A female robotic voice says, *"Welcome to* **Cyberama,** *the best VR game you will ever play!"*

2

HUSTLE IN THE CASTLE

The game has us enter our names and ages. Dave and I enter our details.

"Wait, what are you kiddos doing? Why did you give out your personal information like name and age to an online game?" Cyber Kiki screams.

"Umm, so it'll let us play," I reply.

"You're never supposed to give out your **Personally Identifiable Information**, or **PII**, to strangers, or in this case, a random online game. Your PII includes things like your name, birth date, address, car license plate number, credit card number, and other similar things that belong to you," she replies.

"Well, this is not a random online game, a lot of people I know are playing it. Plus, we already entered it and it's too late," Dave says.

Cyber Kiki doesn't look too happy. She sighs at us and looks at our tablets. She doesn't want to enter her details as player three and wants to stay low, or as she says, incognito.

The game has six levels, each with a different theme—a castle, Wonders of the World, the Metaverse, inside the human body, a magical rainforest, and a race car track. The screen prompts us to choose our avatars. Dave and I select avatars that look like us.

"*Press the 'Start' button to enter Level 1,*" the voice says. We press the start button. We're standing in the courtyard of a real-looking tall castle from ancient times.

"This is HUGE, like a football stadium!" Dave exclaims.

The castle has tall walls made of large, gray bricks, cobblestone flooring, security guards near the main gate, and an iron fence outside the gate. I look up at the vast blue sky, which has just a few clouds, making it look like a bright, sunny morning. On one side of the courtyard is a small garden with a pond and a fountain. The other side has three tall doors, which are closed. Cyber Kiki, Dave, and I are alerted by the loud ring of a bell coming from the clock tower just past the courtyard. The bell rings eleven times. Once the ringing sound disappears from our ears, Cyber Kiki points to the first room on the right.

"Should we enter it?" I ask. Dave, Cyber Kiki, and I enter the room, which looks like the inside of a flight control tower with a bunch of computers and keyboards. There is a giant digital clock counting down from 10:00.

The voice from the game is back.

"Welcome, Maya and Dave! To complete Level 1, you must reach the vault at the center of the castle on the second floor, near the clock tower. However, it's not so easy! You'll have to defeat two bandits, who are also trying to get to the vault to steal the treasure. You have ten minutes to complete Level 1, and there are no second attempts. You win when you capture the reg flag at the end of the level. Good luck!"

"Ten minutes—that's not a lot!" Dave exclaims.

"I know. But we don't have much time to think. Let's get to the action," I reply.

Cyber Kiki directs Dave and me towards a computer screen displaying the security camera, where we notice two bandits, a man, and a woman, dressed in black and white stripes, trying to enter the castle. Cyber Kiki prompts us toward the console to deploy security to the castle.

The castle has three security levels. I press the button that reads "Security Level 1." *Bam!* A large wooden gate drops in front of the castle archway, blocking entry to the bandits. But the bandits only take seconds to cut into the wooden gate with an electric saw and get inside. NO WAY!

Well, that was too easy! I should have known better. Cyber Kiki suggests that I increase the security. "They look like **"bad actors"**, a common term used to refer cybercriminals of all kinds. Let's increase the security to level 2," she says.

As I press the button that reads "Security Level 2," a heavy iron gate drops down in front of the bandits, and the console prompts me to set a password for the gate. I

need to enter something quickly to prevent the bandits from barging into the castle. I hurriedly type "qwerty," the first six alphabet keys on my keyboard. Not surprisingly, the bandits crack the password quickly. As time is running out, I start to panic and press "Security Level 3." A force field door, which everything will bounce off, is installed.

"Hey, I've seen a similar force field door in Mindcraft," says Dave.

"Great, but let's focus; we don't have much time to stop the bandits from getting to the vault!" I reply.

"Okay, okay, go ahead and enter a stronger password this time," suggests Dave. "Actually, enter a long pass-phrase with upper- and lower-case letters, numbers, and symbols. This kind of combination, especially if longer than thirteen characters, can take a million to a trillion years to hack," Cyber Kiki says.

"Really?" I ask.

"I bet it's true. Here, let me try," Dave says as he enters the letters "Le@VeU$Al0ne".

Phew! It's been a few minutes, and the bandits are still not in.

"That worked! We did it!" shouts Dave as he high-fives Cyber Kiki and me.

"Good job, you two! Let's get to the vault now." Cyber Kiki says.

I look up at the screen, and we have only four minutes left! Gulping and gasping, Cyber Kiki, Dave and I run around the castle to get to the vault, for what seems like the longest four minutes of our lives. We run through a courtyard, cross a bridge, pass a hallway, and enter three gates before reaching the vault. The vault has a metal mesh door through which we see treasures.

"OPEN SESAME!" calls Dave. Nothing happens.

"You think that's going to open the door of a vault inside such a big castle?" I sigh, "Here, watch how it's done."

"ABRACADABRA!" We wait—still nothing.

Cyber Kiki pulls up a laser beam that cuts through the metal mesh door. While Dave and I are watching in awe, Cyber Kiki motions for us to rush inside the vault.

"Ooooooo, that was super cool, Cyber Kiki!"

"Thanks, Maya!" says Cyber Kiki as she winks at me.

The vault is about two stories tall, taller than my house. It has shiny flooring and white marble stone walls with intricate gold carving. There's a huge chandelier with rainbow light beaming through the shiny crystals, boxes of treasures on the ground, and expensive-looking armor inside glass cases across the walls.

"Wow, look at all these jewels," I say as I see the boxes on the floor full of rubies, emeralds, sapphires, other precious gemstones, and gold. Next to a shiny ruby is a big red flag. I run and grab the flag. Just then, I see a

blinding flash. Everything disappears, and we're back at the game's main screen. The voice from the game says, *"First flag captured! Congratulations, you have successfully completed Level 1 of the game!"*

"That was something!" I exclaim as I remove my VR goggles.

"See, I told you," says Dave. "I knew you'd like the game. I loved it!"

"And, thanks to Cyber Kiki for the super cool laser move. That was awesome!" I congratulate the proud-looking flamingo.

"I can't wait to tell Mom and Dad about this exciting game," I say. I then turn to Dave. "It's getting late, I'll see you tomorrow, Dave. Maybe we can play Level 2 of *Cyberama?*"

"Maybe? I can't wait till tomorrow evening to see what Level 2 has in store for us!" he replies. I walk him to the door and wave him bye. I then run to the kitchen, where Mom is hurriedly making cheese sandwiches."

"Maya, your dad and I may have had a breakthrough moment in our research. I've got to get back right away. Here is your dinner. We can talk more tomorrow, okay?

I promise." Mom rushes back to her room after she made my dinner.

"Okay Mom, bye!"

I say goodnight to my cyber pals and go to my room to eat my dinner. I can't wait for tomorrow to play *Cyberama* again!

Little do I know, someone is trying to guess the pattern of how I'd set a password.

3

PANDADEMIC

Dave comes over after school the next day so we can play more *Cyberama*. I can tell he is as anxious and excited, as I am. I open my tablet and find a few dialog boxes that display the words "Access Denied."

"Huh? What access, and who denied it?" confused, I look at Dave. "I wonder if someone tried to access my tablet when I was not around."

"Did you have Tech time today at school?" Dave asks.

"No, I didn't. I didn't open my tablet after *Cyberama* last evening."

"Hmmm, why don't you check the last log-in time on your tablet?"

"Good idea!" I say, opening the system settings to look at the last log-in time.

"1:32 AM. Huh?!" I gasp. I pause for a minute. Then I gasp again.

"Maya, what?"

"Hmm…wait, I'll be back," I say as I run to my mom asking if she or Dad tried to login to my tablet. Mom says she didn't, and asks if everything is okay. I say yes and come back to my room.

"The only other person in the room yesterday was Cyber Kiki. She heard me say I needed to change the default password and probably guessed it as 'Iyer123,'" I snarl.

"Oh! I thought the cyber pals were there to protect you. Why would they do that then?"

"I don't know! But I'm not going to trust anyone anymore!"

"Hey kiddos! Last evening was fun, eh?" Cyber Kiki says as she enters the room. "Did you change the default password on your tablet, Maya? I thought of some recommendations for you. A super secure passphrase that even the smartest hacker in the world can't hack!"

Dave and I look at each other.

"Thanks, Cyber Kiki, I got it covered. Dave and I are about to study. Catch you later!"

"Okay, bye. By the way, I told the other bots about *Cyberama*, and Cyber Panda really wants to watch you play Level 2." Cyber Kiki says, as she goes out.

"What? No! I mean, we don't think we need help. We're fine!" I say.

"Help? Did I hear help? Hello, hello! Help is my middle name!" says an animated Cyber Panda, with black circles around his eyes, a round body, and an even rounder belly.

"Hey, Cyber Panda. Aren't you supposed to be... umm... chewing on bamboo, or something?" I ask sarcastically.

"Ha ha! Robots don't eat animal food. We get charged with electricity, and I am super charged today to play *Cyberama* with you both. Let's go!"

"But we don't have any extra VR goggles," says Dave.

"Don't you worry! Maya's parents made us custom VR goggles," an overconfident Cyber Panda replies.

Dave and I look at each other again. I guess there is no getting around it. We look at our tablets and put on our VR goggles. As I enter Level 2, some of the modern wonders of the world are displayed on the main screen, including the Colosseum in Italy, the Taj Mahal in India (which I've actually been to!), the Great Wall of China, and Chichen Itza.

"Wait, I count eight. I thought there were only seven wonders of the world," I exclaim.

"That's what I thought, too. Also, is the Empire State Building even in the modern list of wonders?" Dave asks.

I shrug my shoulders and say, "I'm not sure."

The female voice is back. *"Welcome back, Maya and Dave! In order to play Level 2 of Cyberama, select the wonder of the world on the same continent as you are. **You have a special offer waiting after you finish Level 2.** Good luck!"*

Dave and I select the Empire State building, which is in the United States.

"Great! You're playing from the United States of America. Now, guess how many miles your home is from the Empire State Building," the voice says.

"Fifty! We're about fifty miles from the Empire State Building!" calls out Cyber Panda. I enter fifty.

"Okay, you are playing from the city of New York. Name a famous landmark near your home," asks the voice. Dave and I discuss if we should enter Central Park, Broadway, or the Greenburgh Nature Center. As I type the words "Central Park," Cyber Panda screams.

"*WAIT!!* Don't do it! I have a feeling the game is trying to guess your address. You know it's not safe to give away your home address to an online game, right?" Cyber Panda asks.

"What? No! This is just a game. What will the game do, knowing our home address? Plus, we could have lied about any other continent. What's the big deal anyway?" I ask.

"But you didn't lie! This is called **Social Engineering**. It's a tactic that cybercriminals use to trick you into giving out personal information without even knowing it. You quit the game right now!" Cyber Panda pleads.

"No, we can't quit the game! We have to play to finish Level 2!" says Dave. I nod, passionately agreeing. I enter Central Park, which is two miles from our home.

Cyberama displays five street names and asks us to select the street name to finish Level 2. I choose the correct street name, and a red flag appears on the screen. Dave and I catch the flag, and we successfully finish Level 2.

"*Second flag captured! Congratulations, Maya and Dave! You have completed Level 2,*" says the voice.

"Yay!" I cheer and high-five Dave. Cyber Panda leaves me hanging while glaring at us. "The game now knows the street you live in. If the game's creators are cyber savvy, they can confirm your approximate location with an **IP address** and possibly even hack into street cameras to look for kids your age. Do you even realize that?"

"Cyber Panda, chillax! It's not a big deal. What's an IP address anyway?" I ask.

"It's like your home address, but for a computer. Every computer has a unique address. You're giving away too much information to an online game! You or your parents could end up experiencing **identity theft**," says Cyber Panda.

"An identity what?" Dave asks.

"Identify theft is when someone, like a cybercriminal,

uses someone else's personal information to commit crimes," Cyber Panda replies.

"Okay, Cyber Panda! You're starting to really creep us out. I've noticed that my parents enter our home address on the internet all the time. Mom enters our address for shipping stuff she shops online. Why won't they get in trouble and only us?" I ask

"I'm pretty sure they don't enter the address on the internet all the time, and when they do, it's only on legitimate websites. Even if a stranger shows up at the door knowing the address, they're able to protect themselves. You both are not," Cyber Panda replies.

"Well, I have you pals to protect me! We'll be fine, okay? Now, Dave and I have to talk about homework. We'll catch up with you later, bye!" I say.

Cyber Panda doesn't look pleased but leaves the room with a blank face.

"Cyber Panda is too paranoid. I'm glad you kicked him out," Dave says.

"I feel bad, but yeah, he was starting to creep me out."

Dave and I look at my tablet screen and notice a

pop-up, with an offer to skip a few levels, and upgrade to the premium version of the game.

"*Congratulations! The premium version of* Cyberama *is now available. You can make custom avatars, get extra lives, and connect with players around the world. The premium version is free for a limited time. And if you click within the next hour, we will mail you stickers of your avatars for FREE! You'll be asked to enter credit card information but will not be charged. Click Next to find out more!*"

"Wait what? Who doesn't want free stuff?" asks Dave.

"Hmm, I guess," I say, as we click "Next." The following screen prompts Dave and me to take our pictures using our tablet cameras.

"I don't feel good about taking our pictures and uploading them to the internet. We don't know how they may be used," I say, concerned.

"I think you are right, Maya. We don't want Cyber Panda to creep us out again, do we?"

"I think he exaggerated things. Did he think that cybercriminals would show up at our home or something? Even if they did, what would they do? Steal something? It's not like we're millionaires. This is just a game, and like you said, if everyone is playing it, who has the time to visit a thousand houses and steal, huh?" I say.

Dave smiles uncomfortably. "Let's skip the Premium version. I'm okay with just continuing with the free version for now."

"Yep," I agree as I press *Skip*.

"Hello, hello! It's me again!" Dave and I turn around to that familiar voice and double hello. Of course, it's Cyber Panda.

"Hey, Cyber Panda, are you still here? We didn't give away any personal information. In fact, we just now skipped a great offer from the game!" I say.

"No, I came by to drop off these webcam cover slides for your tablets. May I place them?" asks Cyber Panda. Dave and I both nod. Cyber Panda places the covers and waves bye as he leaves the room.

"Hey, I think we did the right thing by not entering our parents' credit card information. You never know, the card could get hacked, or their money could get stolen," says Dave.

"True, and if Cyber Panda saw us uploading our pictures to this game, he'd freak out, and perhaps say "The game is going to create digital evil twins of you both," I say, giggling. We enter Level 3 of *Cyberama* with big grins on our faces.

4

THE METAVERSE

Dave and I find ourselves inside The **Metaverse** as we enter Level 3. The metaverse looks like a digital version of the real world in another universe. I see a digital version of Times Square in New York City. I wonder if we are seeing a setting in New York City because Dave and I gave that information to the game.

Like the real Times Square, this place looks busy, chaotic, and crowded, with a lot of people. Families with kids, tourists, and people wearing suits. I've seen my dad wear a suit maybe twice in my life. I see giant billboards with flashing colorful screens, fast-moving banners of ads, and movie trailers on billboards! The buildings and people all look digital. I feel the hustle and bustle of Times Square with the noise of taxis, and

the hum and music of street musicians. This chaos is what makes the city so special. This is the coolest thing I've seen in my entire life. I can't wait to tell my class about this. They won't believe me! Unless some of them have already played the game and would have come across this level.

I run around a few blocks in the metaverse version of Times Square.

"Dave, where are you?" I call out as I run.

"Maya! Here! I'm here!"

"Hey, do you think this is why the game was trying to take our pictures?" I ask.

"I don't know..." Dave replies.

We run around a few blocks. Then, Dave and I suddenly halt when we see a giant candy store. I know we won't get real candy in a virtual store, but I definitely want to check out what it looks like. As we are about to enter the store, I notice something unusual when I see two people standing outside. I run closer to see their faces and gasp! The two people look exactly like my parents!

Dave and I are in utter shock! He puts his fingers on

the sides of his forehead and furrows his eyebrows as if he is concentrating hard. He calls it the *Dave Sense*, where he can sense the future. If anything, every time he has *Dave Sense*, it looks like his stomach is upset. Dave opens his eyes and says, "Don't talk to them."

But I can't resist talking to them.

"Mom, Dad, what are you both doing?" I ask. "Did you decide to step inside the game to find out what I'm doing?"

Suddenly, I feel a hand on my shoulder. I turn around, and it's my cyber pal, Cyber Fox.

"What are you doing here?" I ask.

"I heard a gasp in your room and wanted to make sure you were doing okay. Is everything okay?" Cyber Fox asks.

"Umm, yeah, I'm fine," I say as I turn back to my parents. Mom's avatar looks at me and asks, "Maya— Dad and I wanted to make sure you were safe. Hey, listen, we have something to ask you. Do you remember the project that we were working on? We seem to have misplaced the file that has details about the project, and we need it urgently. Do you happen to know where we may have kept it? Could you tell us?"

I'm confused. Why would my parents come inside the game I'm playing, which I thought they didn't know about, and ask for details about the project they've been keeping me away from? Something about this doesn't seem right. Cyber Fox notices my confusion, and after hearing what the avatars say, he pulls me and Dave aside from the avatars that look like my parents.

"Maya," he whispers, "Just before I put on my VR goggles and got in the game, I saw your parents inside their study. They were working on the research. The people you are talking to are not your parents. Someone is trying to trick you into giving details about their research. What if the game creators know what your parents' faces look like from the internet and created avatars that look just like them? Look, your dad's look-alike is standing instead of sitting in a wheelchair. This whole thing looks like a scam. You've got to exit the game, RIGHT NOW!"

I'm shaking at this point. This is exactly how I felt when I saw a rattlesnake in our backyard two years ago.

I turn around, and Dave is also shaking with fear. We remove our VR goggles and exit the game.

"What just happened there?" I ask Dave.

"I don't know! Cyber Fox could be right," he replies. "I'm scared."

"Me too! It's getting late. I'm going to talk about this to my parents first thing tomorrow. I'll see you later, okay?"

"Okay. Bye, Maya," Dave says as he leaves.

Cyber Fox notices that I'm visibly shaking. He hugs me and says, "It's okay, Maya. Get some rest. We'll figure things out tomorrow."

"Hey, thanks for your help today, Cyber Fox."

"That's what I'm here for! Good night. Sleep tight!" Cyber Fox says as he leaves my room.

I'm in disbelief about the crazy adventure that happened today. What if Cyber Fox didn't reach us in time? Were the avatars I was speaking to my parents' digital evil twins? What will my parents say if I tell them about this tomorrow? Will I get into trouble? Will I be banned from playing *Cyberama* and other online games forever? Will my tablet be taken away from me? Will I not get to meet Dave anymore? I'm SO grounded!

5

RANSACKED!

W*AIIIILLLLL!* The next day, I am woken up by the blaring sound of a loud siren. Is that an ambulance? I also hear dogs barking. I wonder why the siren is so loud. I squint at the desk clock next to me and see it's 3:12 AM! I can barely open my eyes. I must have fallen asleep late last night after all that happened. I rub my eyes, turn the lights on, and head to the living room.

There are cops *everywhere!* Some are talking to my parents, and I see more cops looking around the house. The entire living room has been destroyed. Furniture has been flipped, papers are all over, and windows have been broken. *We've been robbed!*

Dad rushes to me and asks, "Maya dear, are you okay?"

"Dad, what's going on? Did someone try to break into our house?"

"Yes, when we were asleep. Thankfully, our neighbors heard a noise after their dog started barking and quickly called the cops. We're not sure what the thieves were after, but surprisingly nothing valuable seems to be missing. It looks like the criminals tried to open the door to our study. They must've heard the cops and left. We're trying to get the camera footage to see if the thieves left behind any clues. Your mom and I are trying to sort things out, but we assure you that no one is in the house. Do you want to stay with us or go back to your room?"

"Umm, I'll probably go back to my room, Dad," I say and go back to my room in shock, after a gentle hug from Dad. I try to sleep, but I can't. I have a weird feeling that this incident is somehow linked to when Dave and I gave our street name while playing *Cyberama*. Was Cyber Panda right after all? He did say that we were giving away too much information and that criminals could use our IT—or IP address—or something like that, to trace our homes. *OH MY!* What am I going

to do now? I was going to tell my parents about seeing their digital lookalikes yesterday in the game, but now this? What will they think of me if I tell them I may have gotten all of us in trouble and put our entire family in danger? Will the cops arrest me if I tell them the truth about the game? I don't think I should tell anyone just yet.

I got us all into this mess, and I feel like I need to fix this now. I've never had so many serious thoughts going through my mind. This is probably the worst thing that has ever happened to me!

I look at the clock, and it's 4:05 AM. I can hear the cops leaving. With much difficulty, I go back to sleep. Tomorrow, I will play *Cyberama* after school, this time to find out who is behind all of this and what they are after!

• • •

It's another long day at school. I can't wait to get home, tell Dave of everything that happened, and try to find more clues from the game and about the people trying to mess up my life.

Dave comes in and asks, "Hey Maya, are you okay? My parents told me there was a robbery at your place? Do you think it could have been…?" he pauses as he raises his eyebrows.

"I've been thinking the same but am too scared to admit it."

"You know, I didn't sleep well last night. I felt that someone was watching me," Dave says.

"Someone may have really been watching me last

night! I think we should play *Cyberama* just to find out if what Cyber Panda said is true," I reply. Dave nods his head in agreement.

We put on our VR goggles to play *Cyberama*.

"*Welcome back, Maya and Dave! Would you like to resume where you left?*" the female voice asks. Dave and I press the resume button. We're back in the metaverse. We run around a few blocks looking for the huge candy store. However, to our dismay, the candy store and the digital version of my parents are missing!

"Are we in the wrong level or something?" Dave asks, perplexed.

"I don't know! Do you think the game realized we were suspicious yesterday and made the digital version of my parents disappear?" I exclaim. He shrugs his shoulder and purses his lips in bewilderment.

The rules of this game are weird, if there are any! We run around some more to find the red flag. After about ten minutes, we spot the red flag on the nineteenth floor of a bright blue building. We take a neon, capsule-shaped elevator to the nineteenth floor and catch the flag.

"*Third flag captured! Congratulations, you have completed Level 3 of the game!*"

Dave and I look at each other and exchange smiles.

"I know we didn't find any hints in Level 3, but we're on a roll! Let's play Level 4. What do you say?" Dave asks.

"I guess," I reply. Just then,

RUMBLE…BANG…ZZZZZ

Dave and I hear a loud rumbling sound. We remove our VR goggles and look outside the window to see a bright lightning streak that almost blinds our eyes. We then hear the buzzing sound of electricity and then the power goes out.

"Nooooooooo!" Dave shouts in disappointment as he looks at me. I feel the exact same way. We anxiously wait for the power to come back. Between the faint light from the streetlights coming through the window and the loud rumble, I can't help but notice how heavily Dave and I are breathing. In about five minutes, the power is back, and I anxiously open my tablet to power it again. I can't load *Cyberama*! I notice a message: "No internet connection."

I click on the small radar icon with circular arcs on my tablet screen to check the internet connection. For some reason, the regular internet network isn't working.

"Something must be wrong with the modem," I say.

"I can't believe we don't get to play *Cyberama*," Dave pouts.

I feel for him; I really like this game too. But, more importantly, I have to find out who's behind all this to keep my family out of harm's way.

6

THE WALL OF FIRE

"I need an internet connection, NOW," I yell.

"Why don't you try to connect to another network?" Dave asks.

We look at the other available networks. "*HomeSweetHome*," "*Trusted_Network*," "*WelcomeToMiCasa*," and "*2fH6j7-Laserjet*" are the ones that show.

"I've seen *HomeSweetHome* before. It's our neighbor's, but it's a secured network, and I don't know the password," I say.

"Yeah, I've seen it before too. I don't know the password either. Same with the Casa one. What about the other two?" Dave asks.

"*Trusted_Network*" is showing as an unsecured network. I saw a warning last week that my tablet's firewall is out of date. A **firewall** keeps checking for strangers and bad actors who are trying to reach us through a network that is not secure or protected. Joining an unsecured network, especially now with an out-of-date firewall, is not a safe choice.

"The last thing I want is to give strangers access to my tablet, though I'm starting to think we already gave them access by playing *Cyberama*! UGH!" I say.

"What's the worst thing that can happen anyway? We really don't know whether us giving away the name of the street we live on to a computer game is the reason your house got robbed. I too entered our street name, and we're neighbors. My house didn't get robbed. Don't we need to play *Cyberama* to find out who's behind all this? If your modem got burned from that lightning, we don't know when it might get fixed. I say we connect to *Trusted_Network*. It looks safe and doesn't require a password," Dave says. He sounds convincing.

Dave then rests his fingers on the sides of his forehead, cringes, wrinkling his eyebrows, and triggers the *Dave Sense*. He then opens his eyes and says, "We're good to go. Click it, I say."

"Hmm, okay. Bad things can't keep happening to us back-to-back, right?" I ask as I connect to *Trusted_Network*.

And we are connected to the internet! Dave and I put on our VR goggles and open *Cyberama*. As we're about to enter Level 4 of the game, my VR goggles start flashing black and white.

"What's going on, Dave? Are your goggles flashing

black and white too? I can't see anything, and my eyes are starting to hurt," I say.

"Not mine!" he replies.

Dave and I quickly remove our goggles and notice that my tablet is filled with pop-ups, which won't stop. It's like a volcano erupted, and chunks of lava and rocks are pouring out nonstop in the form of gray, rectangle pop-ups on my tablet.

"Can you read the message inside the pop-up? I can't tell. The boxes are appearing on top of one another," Dave exclaims.

"I can't tell either, and there seems to be no way to stop these. Oh boy, are we in trouble again," I say. At this point, I'm starting to freak out so much that I never want to be near a tablet or any computer again, like EVER.

I call out to my cyber pals for help. All the pals except Cyber Ella are on chargers.

"Cyber Ella, we need your help, like RIGHT NOW!" I shout.

"Hi Maya, sure! What's going on?" she asks.

Dave and I show her my tablet. Her robotic eyes get

wider, and I see the reflection of the cascading pop-ups in her eyes. After a few clicks on my tablet, she turns to us and says, "There's only one way to stop this. I will have to go inside the tablet's **bootloader mode** and destroy the pop-ups."

"What does bootloader mode even mean?" Dave asks.

"Bootloader mode is when your tablet is trying to start after you turn it on. It's when your computer memory is being checked and applications are loading. It's like when you wake up, your brain sends signals to all the systems to wake up," she says as she puts on a pair of VR goggles.

What happens in the next five minutes, I will never be able to fully explain. Cyber Ella connects to my tablet, flames come from her mouth, and she does a classic Flamethrower move like from the video games. She destroys the pop-ups, one by one, until all of them disappear!

"Is Cyber Ella a Unicorn or a dragon?" Dave whispers into my ear.

"Right? I'm guessing this is one of the superpow-

ers my parents talked about when they introduced the cyber pals. I wonder what other tricks they each have?"

I guess she is creating some sort of a wall of fire to protect us from whoever is sending these pop-ups. I see fiery sparks of yellow-orange fire going all over my tablet screen. As the flames light up the room, I look at Cyber Ella in awe with my left hand covering my mouth. Cyber Ella opens the settings on my tablet and asks me to update the firewall. I immediately click the "Update" button.

"Verifying Updates… Verified… Installing the latest version of the firewall… Please wait."

I wait, as my heart races, knowing we don't have much time. I look at Dave; his eyes are glued to the tablet, his mouth wide open.

Installing Firewall… *10%… 25%… 50%…*

Dave and I exchange anxious looks. He is also taking deep breaths.

75%… 90%… 99%…

Will the installation be complete already? This seems like the longest minute of my life.

100%

Your Firewall is now up to date.

Cyber Ella removes her VR goggles and flashes a smile at Dave and me.

I hug Cyber Ella and say, "Thank you for saving us!"

Dave joins us for a group hug. He then looks at Cyber Ella's face again to check if her mouth is still smoking from all the fire blazing. The three of us laugh out loud.

"That was a close one," I cry, looking at Dave.

"Yes, it was. I'm never going to connect to an unsecured network again, especially if I know my firewall is not up to date," he says. I disconnect from the unsecured network. More time has passed, and it seems like we won't be able to get back to playing *Cyberama* anytime soon.

7

THE PHISHING WISH?

For the next twenty minutes, Dave and I check to see if our regular internet connection—Iyer Manor—is back. I keep wondering why an online game that was supposed to be pure fun is now possibly causing all of these crazy things to happen in my life. After Level 1, I was super excited about boasting to my class about the adventures of Cyberama. Now, I don't want anything to do with the game. In fact, kids in my class would want to stay away from this nerdy girl.

After about thirty minutes, the regular secured network shows up on the list. I click to join it, and we're back on track! We enter Level 4 of *Cyberama*. We are inside a huge, dense, tropical rainforest! Not just any rainforest, but one which looks magical and breathtak-

ing, like from the movies! We look around and see lush greenery, tall trees, creeping vines, and leaves dripping water into a lake. Rays of sunlight shine between the tree tops, and the bright yellow and orange hues start to disappear at the misty layer above the lake. The lake is filled with patches of blue and neon bioluminescence, with jellyfish glowing purple and pink floating around. The sound of a waterfall, chirping birds, and shrieking monkeys is music to my ears. I can hear the rain hitting the leaves above my head. Every plant looks unique and is glistening from the rain. Dave and I are in absolute awe!

"Whoa! What are those?" asks Dave.

"Huh? Ahhhh! Help!" I squeal, looking at the little dragons that are flying around us.

"Don't worry. They're flying up high. They won't bother us," Dave comforts me.

"Knock knock! May I come in?" shouts a voice behind us. Dave and I look at each other, remove our VR goggles, and turn around. It's Cyber Meow!

"Hey, Cyber Meow! Good evening! Wanna join us?" I ask.

"Holy Meow! This place looks beautiful!" Cyber Meow exclaims. Dave and I smile at each other.

At that moment, the female voice returns *"Welcome to Level 4 of Cyberama! In this level, you must catch one thousand points worth of fish and overcome obstacles. You do not have any spare lives. Good luck!"* The voice fades out.

For the next few minutes, Dave, Cyber Meow, and I look around and catch all kinds of fish from the lake —goldfish, guppies, blobfish, catfish, stingray, and even tiny swordfish. We then look at the screen to determine how many points we've collected.

"Only forty points for all the hard work?" Dave exclaims. I agree with him. It's like we've been catching fish forever.

"Maybe the fish don't all have the same number of points," Cyber Meow says.

"Hey! Look there!" I shout, pointing to a huge blue whale closer to the other side of the lake. "Let's go catch it!"

As Dave, Cyber Meow, and I get closer to the whale, we see the words "100,000 POINTS" floating around the whale.

"One hundred thousand points??!!" Dave exclaims.

"Oh, my goodness! That'll get us to the finish line right away. Let's go click it." I say.

"Wait, no... no..." Cyber Meow stops me from clicking, "Maya, I don't think you should click on that whale. This looks fishy, too good to be true."

Dave and I laugh. "Yes, Cyber Meow, remember, we are catching fishy things in this level?" Dave says.

"That's not what I meant. This might be a **whale phishing attack**, which cybercriminals use to trick you into clicking something that appears attractive but is actually harmful," she explains.

"Hey, we can't win the game without clicking on anything. They don't design games that way, okay." I argue with Cyber Meow. I don't listen to her and click on the big, fat whale.

BOOM! BANG!

Suddenly, all the fish that Dave, Cyber Meow, and I have collected disappear, and our score is back to zero!

"What just happened? The whale said one hundred

thousand points, and I clicked on it. Why did all our points go back to zero? This is cheating!" I cry.

"Told ya! It was a whale phishing attack. Let me see if I can retrieve some of our lost points. Hang in there," Cyber Meow says as she searches around the lake. She tries hard but can't find the fish.

"Don't worry, Maya, it's a game. We can catch fish again," Cyber Meow comforts me.

"*AAAAAAAHHHHHH! GHOST!*" Dave screams in horror and removes his VR goggles. Cyber Meow and I remove our VR goggles and look at Dave, who is still looking at the tablet.

GULP! I scream in horror too! The three of us look at each other. None of us are touching anything, and yet the mouse pointer in the game suddenly starts moving all by itself!

8

BAM! IT'S A SCAM

"That can't be a ghost!" Cyber Meow says, "I think that Maya clicking on that big whale gave the creators of the game access to her tablet."

"What does that mean?" I ask, in shock.

"I think I know what it means," Dave says, "Remember, we learned about phishing, a type of social engineering. It's a method **cybercriminals** use to trick people into clicking something, so they can get access to a computer and do bad things."

"That's right! Wait, did I just get phished?" I exclaim.

"Yep, girl, you did!" Cyber Meow says. "Phishing is just one of the methods of getting access to someone's computer. **Pharming**, **smishing**, and **vishing** are some other ways. In pharming, harmful code or a program is installed on someone's computer, which sends them to a fake website. It's like someone giving you wrong directions intentionally. In smishing, cybercriminals send a text message to a cell phone, tricking people into clicking on a harmful link."

"Shouldn't it be called Tishing then?" Dave asks.

"Nope, the word Smishing comes from **SMS**, which is another name for text messaging," Cyber Meow explains. "Vishing is carried out over the phone, where the goal is to trick you into providing information or clicking a link to install malware on your computer, or to gain access to your tablet... like what just happened."

"Huh? What do we do now?" I ask worriedly.

"Let's disconnect from the internet, restart the tablet, and see if they still have access to your tablet. I'm not sure if that'll fix the issue, but let's try," Cyber Meow says. We restart the tablet and wait for a few minutes. The mouse pointer is no longer moving.

Phew! Dave and I breathe a huge sigh of relief.

"Maya, Dave, it seems like the creators of *Cyberama* want something from you. There's only one way to find out what it is. Finish Level 4. C'mon, let's catch every itty-bitty fish out there," Cyber Meow suggests.

"Unless you eat any along the way, kitty!" Dave says, winking at Cyber Meow.

Despite the trouble we are in, I smile and continue to catch fish with Dave and Cyber Meow. After about ten minutes, we have enough to finish the level. Another giant blue whale appears, this time holding a red flag.

"Ouch, should I catch the flag, Cyber Meow?" I ask.

"I think we've finished the level. Go for it!"

I catch the flag, and a blinding flash appears.

"*Fourth flag captured! Congratulations, you've completed Level 4 of Cyberama!*" the female voice is back.

Dave removes his VR goggles and is about to leave when...

KNOCK KNOCK

"C'mon in," I call. And—It's *MOM*!

Dave and I panic a bit and rush to cover the tablet screen with our backs, so Mom can't see it.

"What's going on, you two? Why do you look so shocked?" Mom asks.

"No, nothing, Mom! What's up?" I ask with a fake smile.

"Hmm, okay. Listen, Maya, are you playing an online game called *Cyberama*?" she asks.

I instantly freeze. THAT'S IT! Mom knows! I was planning on telling her and dad about the game, but so much has happened that I don't even know where to start. I wish I could somehow disappear right now. Perhaps the criminals can just suck me into the tablet because I'm going to be in trouble anyway!

I try hard not to show my emotions on my face, gather up my courage, and ask, "Why do you ask, Mom?"

"I just received an unusual email from a game called *Cyberama*, with a link to pre-order the sequel of the game. I haven't heard of the game and wasn't sure what to do with it. So, I thought I'd come and check with you," Mom says.

"Yes, Mom. *Cyberama* is the VR game I told you about."

"Okay. Does this game have a chat room?" mom asks.

"Oh—no, Mom."

"Alright. I didn't completely read the email, but if you have any issues with the game, let me or Dad know. Bye sweetie!"

"Sounds good. Bye, Mom!"

Dave, Cyber Meow, and I breathe a huge sigh of relief!

"Phew, I feel so much better now that Mom knows I'm playing *Cyberama*. I still need to explain everything to my parents, but I'll do it after finding who is behind all of this. Thanks, Cyber Meow, for not ratting us out."

"Rats—and ratting out people—are two things I

don't like to do!" she says, smiling. "Maya, did you provide your mom's email address to the game?"

"I did not!"

"Hmm, in that case, I wonder if the game creators
searched through your tablet files to find your mom's
email address, which is bad! I wonder if the cybercriminals were meaning for your mom to click the email to
get access to her computer?" Cyber Meow warns.

Dave and I look at each other in shock.

"The game must have a copy of the email. Let's look
in the Messages folder of the game," she says.

Cyber Meow finds a copy of the email from the
Messages folder, opens it, and gasps. The message reads
*"Dear player, since you enjoyed playing Cyberama part 1,
we think you'll enjoyed Cyberama part 2. Click Upgrade
NOW to downloaded the game for FREE. We could not
verify your billing address, and credit card number, so please
enter them."* She points out how the email meets several
characteristics of a phishing email and warns Dave
and me not to click the link to pre-order the sequel.
The message is addressed to "Dear Player," which is
generic and not specific. The message creates urgency,

Subject: FOR CYBERAMA PLAYERS!

From: cyberamateam@cyber.com

To: tarascientist@email.com

Dear Player,

Since you enjoyed playing *Cyberama Part 1,* we think you'll enjoy *Cyberama Part 2.* Click Upgrade NOW to downloaded the game for **FREE**. We could not verify your billing address, and credit card number, so please enter them.

REPLY   FORWARD   PRINT

asking the reader to upgrade immediately. The message even has grammatical mistakes like "enjoyed" and "downloaded"! Finally, the message asks for personal information, like home address and credit card number. When we hover over the "Upgrade NOW" button, the link has an unrelated website address that reads "www. cyberama5837ru683-hd78204.com"

This time, I know better than to click on suspicious links. Clicking the big blue whale didn't do me any good. Cyber Meow selects the message and clicks, "Delete Forever."

"Okay, it's getting late. I'm going to leave now before my mom asks me questions. I'm done answering questions today!" Dave says as he leaves home.

"Good night, Dave. Good night, Cyber Meow," I say.

9

INSIDE THE
HUMAN BODY

The next evening, as Dave and I are about to enter Level 5 of Cyberama, my cyber pal Cyber Owl comes in and intervenes before we can start.

"Maya, Dave, I think you should stop playing this game. A lot of bad things have been happening in your lives, including your house getting robbed, since you and Dave started playing the game. I don't feel good about it." Cyber Owl cautions.

"What? No! Dave said everyone is playing it. Everyone in our school plays online games all the time. Some even play during class! Why do they even make online games if they're not meant to be played, huh?

Dave and I have been the good kids sticking to the "**screen time**" routine. Good kids deserve to have some fun!" I argue. This is perhaps the most I've spoken in a single breath!

"Not every online game is bad, Maya, but this one has constantly been asking for your personal information from the beginning, from what the other bots say. Your house just got robbed, for goodness' sake! What more signs do you need to tell you to stop playing the game?" Cyber Owl asks, his tone starting to get more serious. "The right thing to do would be just to tell your parents about everything. Let's go!"

"Hey, no fair! Please, Cyber Owl, if the game is indeed the reason for the bad things happening in my life, shouldn't I find out who is behind all this? Just one more level? Please, I promise! I'm sure we'll find hints in Level 5. Pretty please?" I beg.

"Okay, you can play the game on one condition. I'll be the main player in Level 5. You and Dave will just be watching me play, okay?" Cyber Owl asks with a sigh.

Dave and I look at each other. Since we don't have much of a choice, we agree to the proposal, put on our

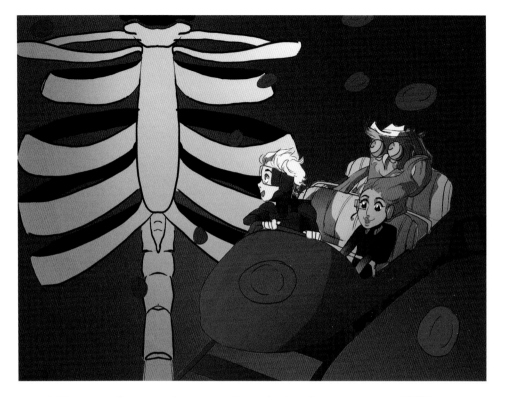

VR goggles, and enter Level 5 of *Cyberama*. We're inside A HUMAN BODY!

CLICKETY-CLACK…off we go on a roller coaster!?

"AAAHHH" Dave and I yell, trying hard to buckle our seat belts. I see a lot of red and pink slime dangling around me. I look further up and see that it is hanging from—a rib cage? I turn around and see muscles, fibers, and blood. The red blood cells are floating around like tiny round chunks of lucky charms. This looks so cool, like a living, human body, but also a bit icky! I'm not the

type who likes things wet and slimy, but Dave enjoys catching toads occasionally. I turn around and see Dave enjoying the ride, with his hair flying around.

The game voice is back. "Welcome to Level 5 of *Cyberama*. You must catch red blood cells from each body part to finish the level. Good luck!"

"Woot, woot! Let's have some fun, shall we?" Cyber Owl asks.

"Finally! We thought you'd never warm up to us and that you don't like having fun, ever!" Dave exclaims.

Cyber Owl laughs and steers the roller coaster near the body's stomach. As Dave and I extend our arms to catch the floating red blood cells, Mr. Scowl Owl pulls up a transparent screen in front of us, presses a few keys, and hits a button that says "Launch." A small, squiggly, brown centipede-like digital **worm** is launched.

"What are you doing, Cyber Owl? Is that something you ate last night that didn't sit well in your stomach?" Dave asks and giggles. I giggle too. Dave can be pretty funny, but usually, I just find him silly. Sometimes he's gross.

"Just sit back, relax, and enjoy the show!" Cyber Owl replies in a mysterious tone.

As we watch, the worm keeps multiplying itself to breach into the walls of the stomach.

"WAAAIT, these worms look like computer worms, the ones that keep multiplying themselves to slow down a computer until it eventually crashes. We've got to stop the worms before they damage the red blood cells or even the entire body. Unless—" I sigh.

"Unless what," asks a confused Dave.

"Unless, Cyber Owl, you're trying to launch worms to slow down the game and eventually crash it?" I ask, looking at Cyber Owl.

"You know, Maya. You aren't too bad for the average twelve-year-old. I'm impressed," he replies.

Dave and I look at each other, nodding our heads from left to right. Then we scream, "NOOOOO!"

Then, something odd happens. Something that shocks even Cyber Owl.

10

THE POP-APP

A pop-up comes in the game asking us to install an **Antivirus** update to protect the files on the tablet.

"Seriously? I haven't seen this many pop-ups in my entire life," I say.

"POP-A-RAAMAA!" Dave sings. He and I laugh while Cyber Owl looks at the tablet.

"ARGH, the game must have realized it's being breached and is trying to deploy an **Anti-malware** update to destroy the worms," he scowls again.

"I've heard of antivirus. What is anti-malware?" I ask.

"A virus is just one type of **malware**, which is harmful software trying to do bad things to your computer. This pop-up is tricking you into clicking it, so it can actually

harm your computer. Malware is short for malicious software." Cyber Owl replies.

"Okay. Know what, Cyber Owl? Now I really think you're blabbering. The pop-up doesn't look fake. We must install the update. What if something bad happens if we don't, and we possibly get stuck inside this level, like forever?" I ask.

"Maya, no. This pop-up could be malware in disguise. Don't fall for it!" Cyber Owl warns.

"Hey, my tablet, my rules! And—MAYA RULES!" I stomp.

"Remember what we decided? I play Level 5, and you both watch!" Cyber Owl pushes me away and closes the pop-up.

"HEY! That is so not cool!" I say.

Cyber Owl doesn't listen and steers the roller coaster towards the brain. I'm now starting to get mad at Cyber Owl and wondering if he is a cyber pal or a cyber villain himself! He pulls up the transparent screen again, presses a few keys, and hits "Launch." What's he going to launch this time? A snake? A bazooka?

Neither! A wooden horse is launched, which heads straight towards the brain.

"Maya, you know what this is, right," Dave asks.

"Oh—my—horse! It's a **Trojan horse**, a deadly virus that can erase a computer's **memory** and is difficult to destroy. I knew Cyber Owl was up to something villainy, again!"

"Are you trying to erase the information the game has stolen from us, like our address?" Dave asks.

Cyber Owl looks at Dave and winks.

BOOM! THUD! JOLT! Suddenly, our roller coaster starts shaking! I hold on tightly to Cyber Owl and

Dave, and turn around. It's Cyber Fox! Wait, is another super villain joining the show? I start to freak out. This is worse than when Dave dressed up as a Dilophosaurus for Halloween and had no clue how to say it.

However, something shocking happens. Cyber Fox pushes Cyber Owl off the driver seat, steers the roller coaster off the track, and crashes through the Trojan horse. Sparks start flying all around as soon as the coaster hits the horse, and a mini digital explosion occurs. Within seconds, the horse disappears into thin air.

11

REALWARE OR MALWARE?

"**W**hat are you doing, Cyber Fox? Are you nuts?" asks a mad Cyber Owl.

"Hey, hey, hey—calm down, Cyber Owl," I call.

"Nuts? Me? What's wrong with you? Malware and viruses are pretty bad and should never be used on other people," says a calm Cyber Fox. Finally, someone to talk sense into this crazy owl.

"Don't act like you don't know what's happening! Cybercriminals are trying to hack into Maya's tablet and steal information. We must protect her and her parents," Cyber Owl snarls.

"Excuse me, hello," yells Dave raising his hand.

"Ah yes, and you, Dave," Cyber Owl continues. "The only way to defeat these cybercriminals is to hack back into the game, and ultimately, into their system."

"But that's wrong!" Cyber Fox exclaims.

"Nope! All is fair in war! I'm ethically hacking. I know how to hack into computers, and I'm just using my skills to defeat the bad actors," Cyber Owl replies.

"Like a good cop!" Dave finishes.

"Exactly!" Cyber Owl smiles in pride.

"Wait, but are you a hacker?" I ask.

"Not a regular hacker, but an **ethical hacker**—one who uses cyber skills to save the world from evil. See, that's why I have my white hat on; I'm a **White Hat Hacker**," Cyber Owl replies.

"Is that why the criminals outside the castle in Level 1 had black hats?" Dave asks me.

"Hmm, I guess… Makes sense now," I reply.

"There are **White Hat, Gray Hat, Black Hat, Blue Hat, Green Hat,** and **Red Hat hackers**. Some are good, while some are bad. Some hack for money and fame, while some want to seek revenge. Some others are newbies trying to learn to hack," Cyber Owl explains.

"This is crazy! You're acting crazy and teaching these kids that it's okay to do bad things, like hacking," Cyber Fox warns.

Cyber Owl and Cyber Fox start fighting like a pair of three-year-olds. I didn't know robots could fight, although Dad did warn that these bots have feelings.

"Guys! Stop this right now!" I shout. "We're on a mission here, and you guys are fighting like—like a bunch of monkeys!"

"Wait, there's a monkey bot? Is it Cyber Chimp? Or Cyber Ape?" asks Dave.

"What? No, shhh, Dave. Help me make these guys stop fighting," I say.

"Cyber Fox, was what Cyber Owl did wrong?" Dave asks.

"Yes! It's not right to hack into other people's computers. What did your parents do when thieves broke in the other day, Maya?" Cyber Fox asks.

"Called the cops," I answer.

"Exactly! When criminals attack you, you tell the cops, in this case, the cyber police," Cyber Fox says.

WHOA! The roller coaster shakes again. We turn around, and Cyber Owl is missing!

WHOOOOSH.... He is flying super-fast! I mean, he is a bird, but I didn't realize this birdy bot could fly!

"Ush! Cyber Owl is showing off his supersonic speed powers. C'mon kiddos! Hold on tight. Let's follow him," Cyber Fox says as he steers the roller coaster towards the eyes. As we get closer to Cyber Owl, he pulls up his transparent screen, hits a few keys, and…

"I know what's gonna happen next!" Dave yells. "He's

going to launch something uber villainish…something hackilious…"

Dave is right. Cyber Owl launches a pair of binoculars to spy through the eyes of the body.

"That's **spyware**!" I say. The spyware scans through the eyes of the body and pulls up an image.

"Huh? Did the spyware just detect a hole in the game?" asks a surprised Cyber Fox.

"Uhdewnuu," Dave mumbles. I think he meant to say, "I don't know." You know you've known someone long enough when you can decode their mumble jumble.

IMAGE DETECTED. The spyware detects an image that is trying to load on Cyber Owl's transparent screen.

Loading…. 25%……. 50%…………. 100%

Dave yells as soon as he sees the image.

"NOOOOO!" Dave screams again. All of us turn to Dave.

"What is it, Dave?" I ask. I can feel my eyebrows touching the top of my forehead out of curiosity. I've never seen Dave this shocked since the night we finished touring the Haunted House!

"Maya, listen, I have a confession to make," Dave

says, "Remember I told you that everyone's playing *Cyberama*? I—I kinda lied about it!"

"What do you mean you lied? And why would you lie? How did you even know about this game?" I ask.

"I found the flyer on the bulletin board of my Chess club. The flyer mentioned that the first ten people to download the game would win a brand new *GameStation*. However, to win the *GameStation*, the player has to play till the end of *Cyberama*, along with a second player," Dave says.

"WHAT?" I yell. By this time, my eyebrows have shot into my hair. Cyber Owl, Cyber Fox, and I nearly forget to look at the detected image.

GASP! DOUBLE GASP! TRIPLE GASP! We gasp aloud while looking at the image on the screen!

12

IT'S A TRAP

The image on the computer screen shows a picture of Dave, with the address of his chess club below.

"Dave, why is your picture on this computer?" I growl, "Why would you do this to me, Dave?" Look at how much trouble YOU got me into. My house was robbed; we could have been killed. UGH! I can't believe you did this to me. I don't know who to trust anymore!"

"Hey, wait! I had no idea this game would be so creepy. I just thought it's like any other video game for kids," Dave argues.

"Don't say a word! This game has caused so much trouble in my life. What am I going to tell my parents?"

"Maya, calm down. I know you're mad," Cyber Fox says. He turns to Dave.

"Dave, this is really strange. Plus you could have been **doxed**!"

"I could have been what?" Dave asks nervously.

"**Doxing** or **doxxing** is when someone can expose your PII on the internet, including your image, location or any other documents that could reveal your identity. You don't know how many copies of your image may have been uploaded to the internet, and to what websites. Did the flyer say anything else? Do you still have the flyer?" Cyber Fox asks.

"I don't know where I put it. I was too excited to play the game!" Dave replies. He then turns to me and says, "Maya, please tell me Cyber Fox is lying when he says my image could have been uploaded to random websites on the internet!"

"I don't know who is telling the truth anymore. I know you are not!" I reply in anger.

I still can't believe that of all the people I know, my best friend would be the one to trick me into playing this creepy game—just so he could win a GameStation!

"This is like **adware**, a type of software that displays advertisements, tricking people into clicking the ads to provide personal information or download another piece of software. Many times, those who are collecting your information often sell it to others for money. Or once they get the user to download something, they get malware on their computer. In this case, cybercriminals used the flyer to trick Dave and you into downloading the game *Cyberama*," Cyber Fox explains.

"Worm, virus, spyware, and now adware. I wonder what's next?" a surprised Dave asks.

I look at Dave with fury in my eyes. He looks back at me with an apologetic, silly grin. He holds my hand and says, "I'm sorry, Maya! I was the one who got you into all this mess, but you know what? I'll be on your side, along with your super-intelligent cyber pals, until we figure this out, okay?"

"Okay, okay," I reply, trying to smile. I'm still mad at Dave, but he's been my best friend for years. As Dave and I are making up, we hear a whoosh that sounds familiar. It's the same noise that came from Cyber Owl when he launched himself like a rocket last time.

"Oh boy, what's this bird up to now?" screams Cyber Fox, as Cyber Owl seems to be heading towards the hands. Cyber Fox steers the roller coaster, and we follow Cyber Owl. Cyber Owl is tying the arms of the person.

He sees us nearing him and says, "I'm sending a message to the creators of *Cyberama* threatening to destroy the game if they don't reveal their identity. That should show 'em who they're fighting against!"

"Wait—I know what this is," Dave says. "It's a classic **Ransomware** attack. This happens when someone steals information from you or prevents you from using your computer and threatens to destroy it unless you pay them money. Cyber Owl is instead asking for the gamer's identity."

Cyber Fox quickly rushes to untie the arms of the person. He and Cyber Owl are about to fight again.

"Not again! C'mon folks! Remember we've got to stand together to fight the bad actors?" I say.

"I know. I know," says Cyber Fox, as he puts one hand on the right shoulder of Cyber Owl. He turns to Cyber Owl and says, "Listen, if we finish Level 5, we might get more clues about the identity of the creators of the game.

Cyber Owl takes a deep breath, sighs, and says, "Fine!" and agrees to finish Level 5. He then uses his supersonic power to collect red blood cells from all parts of the body in just five minutes! We complete level 5 after Cyber Owl catches a red flag near the mouth.

We ended up catching much more than red blood cells in this level—a huge lie, Dave's image appearing randomly in the game, and the original identity of Cyber Owl as an ethical hacker.

A few minutes later, the voice from the game comes back and says, "*Fifth flag captured. Congratulations, you have completed Level 5 of the game!*"

"Yayyyy!" all of us yell in unison. Dave and I remove our VR goggles.

"Okay, kiddos, it's getting late. Cyber Owl and I are going to head back now. Be safe, okay?" Cyber Fox waves at Dave and me.

"Goodnight, Cyber Owl, Cyber Fox. Maya, I'm so sorry again. I'll never do this to you ever again. Promise! I'll see you tomorrow after school, okay?" says Dave.

"What if I say not okay? Why don't you stay for some more time? Don't you want to play the last level of *Cyberama*?" I ask.

His voice becomes anxious. "I'm not sure what hints we found—it almost seems like we gave away more power to the criminals. Hey, what happens after we finish Level 6?"

"I don't know. I guess the only way to find out is to play," I say. We put on our VR goggles, enter Level 6, and are inside a racecar game.

The female voice is back. "*Welcome to Level 6 of*

Cyberama. *Choose a theme for the racetrack and your cars to play the race. Whoever finishes first after ten laps wins. Good luck!"*

13

THE CYBER BULLY

Dave and I choose the Mountain theme for the racetrack. The scene looks like somewhere from outside of the city of Los Angeles. There are clear blue skies with hardly any clouds, tall palm trees in the middle of dark gray roads on a highway, and billboards showing advertisements. The tall buildings with shiny square windows reflect sunlight, and a huge red bridge is in front of us with greenish, brown mountains in the distance.

"Are you ready to race me at the track, huh?" Dave asks me with a smirk.

"Well, let's see. The real question is if YOU are ready to be beaten by my turbocharged engine with 700 horse-power that can go up to 200mph." I challenge Dave as I pick my pink sports car. The car has a shiny body with just enough tint of candy pink, soft black wheels with metal spikes, and an engine designed to race.

"Bring it on!" says Dave. He chooses a glossy, dark blue sports car. It also has a V8 engine.

I feel nervous. My hands are holding the steering wheel, and I can feel them shaking. I usually don't enjoy racing games, but it's important that I win this one, since my family's safety depends on it.

VROOOM, Dave and I rev up our engines, looking at each other from our cars.

As our cars get ready for the green light, a person in the game waves a black and white checkered flag, indicating *GO!*

3...2...1 SCREEEEEEECH.... Off we go for the challenge. Our cars move through a thick cloud of white and gray smoke. Dave and I focus intensely as we drive through twists and turns around the tall buildings and shining billboards.

Three laps into the game, a message pops up on Dave's screen.

"SpeedRacerX would like to chat with you." A message reads, "Hey there! New to *Cyberama*? Wanna play a private game?"

"Umm, no thanks," says a dismissive Dave as he and I look at each other, shaking our heads left and right.

He ignores the messages from the player. After about one more lap, the player messages again.

"Are you there?"

Dave ignores it.

"Are you scared you'll lose? Do you not have what it takes to play?"

"C'mon, you aren't a coward, are you? You're never gonna win!"

Dave and I look at each other again. We both know not to entertain strangers, especially on the internet, because you never know who's behind the screen! Dave continues to ignore the messages, but more messages keep coming.

"Just do something for me, and I'll be out of your way. If you don't, I'll send mean messages about you for all the players of *Cyberama* around the world to see. The choice is yours!"

"Do what? If I give in and do what the player says,

there's no guarantee that he or she might come back and ask me to do more things. I don't feel right about this at all," Dave says.

The player starts sending mean messages, via chat, to Dave.

We're about five laps into the game. Two more players huddle around Dave with their cars, locking him in the middle. Dave tries to look at me, but I can hardly see him through the other players. We think that SpeedRacerX is trying to be a bully—a cyberbully. Cyberbullies can be convincing and often use fear to make you do things you don't feel comfortable doing.

After about five minutes, the players leave Dave alone. Dave rushes to catch up with me. I can see he's trying hard to tell me something.

"We need to stop playing this game, NOW!" he says.

"What? Why? We're only halfway and have to finish playing the final level!"

"You're not going to believe what the players in the game asked me to do. They wanted me to ask you to share copies of files from Project X that your parents are working on," he says.

"*WHAT?!* How do these players in a random online game know about the project my parents are working on?" I stutter. I now recall the characters in the metaverse level asking me to share files of the project my parents have been working on!

"Wait, this all makes sense now, or at least most of it. I don't think this is an ordinary online game, Maya. I think the players knew about this project and wanted to get information about it. They somehow thought they could probably get that from you. We need to tell your parents now! Like, right now!" he explains. Just then, Dave's car is hit by one of the players, and before I know it, the two players are back around Dave's car.

Dave, the two players, and I are entering a tunnel. I can't see Dave anymore.

BOOM... CRASH... THUD

SpeedRacerX is right beside me. **SMASH!** SpeedRacerX hits my car's front tire, which goes whirling off my car. My car starts spinning. **AAAAAHHHH! HELP!** I am completely lost—my car is spinning—and so is my head. I have no idea what to do!

I'm in utter shock at all that's happening right now.

My car eventually stops spinning, but I can't drive it anymore. Just then, a lightbulb forms in my head. I remove my VR goggles and call on all my cyber pals to help! Yes, all of them. One by one, Cyber Kiki, Cyber Panda, Cyber Ella, Cyber Owl, Cyber Fox, and Cyber Meow all put on their VR goggles, get into the game, and join the racetrack to save Dave from the cyberbullies. Cyber Kiki makes a quick pitstop to change the tires of my car.

BOOM…BANG…THUD…CRASH…SCREECH!

I can't see well anymore because the racetrack is filled with gray and white smoke. I still hear cars crashing, and I'm getting even more anxious. My heart is racing, both inside the game and in real life. Suddenly, I see a player flying in the air. Their car flips over multiple times before it hits the pavement. As soon as the car hits the ground, it catches fire.

I gasp in horror. Could that be Dave? I race faster and try to get closer to the pool of cars. Another car gets kicked out of the pool.

THUD…BOOM…CRASH…SCREECH!

The next few minutes are hazy—tires are rolling, and

more smoke appears. Loud noises are making me dizzy. After an *EPIC* battle of good over evil, I see all my cyber pals and Dave emerge out of the smoke with a sense of victory and pride. I can't stop smiling! I feel like I grew a cape, and these cyber pals are our sidekicks. Okay, fine—it's more like they're the heroes in this scene.

"Oh my! I was so worried about you. I'm so glad you are safe!" I cry.

"So, who won the game, you or Maya?" Cyber Kiki asks Dave.

"Both of us beat the cyberbully, thanks to you all!" Dave laughs as he thanks the cyber pals for saving him from the cyberbullies.

14

SPYING ON THE SPIES

I take off my VR goggles and hug Dave.
"I'm so sorry I put your life in danger," Dave says.

"No, I'm sorry I got you into all this mess because of this project my parents are working on."

"Listen, kiddos. This game has got way out of hand. Maya, you have to uninstall the game right now," Cyber Panda warns.

"But how can we? We haven't finished it. Worse, we don't have any clue how to catch the cybercriminals," Dave says.

"Let me see what I can do," Cyber Panda says as he looks through the game's settings. "Huh, I can't trace the location of the criminals with the IP address," he says.

"WAIT!" Dave exclaims as if he just had a lightbulb moment. "I'll be back!" he says as he rushes to leave my room. After some time, Dave returns with the original flyer, where he found out about *Cyberama.*

"It was in my chess bag. I just remembered!"

I hold the flyer against the light and spot a faint logo.

Cyber Kiki takes a picture of the logo and searches the internet for a potential match. A few search results appear showing possible locations of the logo image, including one result in New York.

"29237 Hartsdale Ave, Suite 500, NY. Wait, this place is close to where we live," I say. "We have to go there NOW!"

"What? Are you crazy?" Cyber Panda yells, and then sighs. "But I can see why you feel that way. If you MUST go, we are going with you."

"No, please, Cyber Panda. I know you are trying to help, but please let Dave and me find some hints. I'm not sure how people will react to robots coming with us. It'll gather attention. Dave and I want to stay low in this operation."

"Well, we can't let you two go alone. Come with me.

I'll use my supersonic power to get you at the location faster than you can imagine," Cyber Owl says.

"That's right, I forgot about that! Do all of you bots have superpowers? What about you, Cyber Meow?" Dave asks.

"I can become invisible," Cyber Meow replies.

"Really? That's so cool!" I say.

"Nope, I was just kidding. Superpowers are so overrated. Why does everybody need to have a superpower? I'm just me, and aren't I super enough?" replies Cyber Meow with a smirk.

"Well sai—" Cyber Owl grabs Dave and me by our shoulders before I finish my sentence. He flies away faster than the speed of sound.

WHOOSH…Off we fly with him!

I blink and open my eyes, and we're at Hartsdale Avenue, in front of a tall black building with thirty-odd floors! I catch a breath, move my messy hair from my face, and see Dave's hair sticking out like a porcupine.

We enter the building, which looks like a regular office building with a front desk and a security guard wearing navy a blue uniform. He has a handheld metal

detector and gun in his pocket. A gun! There's a crowd of people behind the security.

"Suite 500 must be in fifth floor. Now how do we get past the security," I ask nervously.

"Look at that!" Dave says pointing to a banner. Cyber Owl and I look above the crowd to a banner that reads, "WELCOME TO THE VIDEO-GAME CHARACTER CONTEST."

"Wait, does *Cyberama* own the entire building?" I ask curiously.

"I don't know, but I have an idea. Here, follow my lead," Dave says, pulling me and Cyber Owl to the reception.

"We're here for the video-game character contest. Here is our entry," he says, pointing to Cyber Owl.

The security guard examines Cyber Owl, looking at him from head to toe with scrutiny. He then says, "Wow, the character looks so real! Did you two create this?" He starts pinching and pulling Cyber Owl by his cheek.

"Ouch! That hurts!" Cyber Owl yells.

"He even sounds like a real owl! Your entry has a

good chance of winning the contest. Good luck!" he says, letting us in.

"Thank you, sir!" Dave says.

"Attaboy! Now quick, you two go to the fifth floor. I'll make sure no one follows you. Be safe!" Cyber Owl says.

Dave and I slowly sneak out to the fifth floor. The fifth floor is relatively small, with a dark gray carpet, white walls, and four offices with glass doors. Lights are off in all the offices, except one. We see a man and a woman wearing black suits before entering the office. We move closer and hear the words "Project X" and my parents' names!

"*GULP!*" Dave exclaims.

"*SHUSH!*" I try to calm him down. The lady standing outside the office turns around, hearing the shush. Dave, and I quickly pull our heads behind the stairs. Before we know it, Cyber Owls grabs us by our shoulders, and we are back at my home!

"Thanks, Cyber Owl! That was—SUPERSONIC!" Dave exclaims.

"I was concerned, so I followed you both," Cyber Owl replies.

I thank Cyber Owl, go back to my room, log into my tablet and uninstall *Cyberama*.

I then take my cyber pals' advice and knock on my parents' doors to tell them everything that happened. Dave wants to stay by my side.

My parents are shocked but try to listen to me with patience. I mention the game, everything that has happened, and how with the help of our cyber pals, Dave and I prevented the cybercriminals from stealing information about Project X. I also pull up the flyer and mention the location of the cybercriminals. Mom and Dad look at each other in surprise. Mom sits next to Dad, and they take deep breaths. Suddenly, I feel a huge sigh of relief! I'm not scared anymore. I'm okay if my parents are mad at me. After all, I did unintentionally get them into trouble. After a few minutes, my mom speaks.

"Maya, Dave. Thanks for letting us know about *Cyberama* and the criminals. It must have been hard going through all of this and not being able to share it with us. While it wasn't safe for both of you to reveal so much personal information to an online game, we understand this game was specifically designed to get you to reveal personal information, unlike regular games. We're so glad you finally decided to tell us!" she says.

My eyes fill with tears. I hug my mom and dad, and apologize to them for putting the entire family in danger.

"It's okay, princess. We're just glad you are both safe!" Dad says, "Thank you for protecting the information about Project X. Now, Mom and I have a few calls to make."

Dave and I wait outside their room. We can hear them call the Federal Bureau of Investigation, or the FBI of the U.S. Government to report the criminals, the creators of *Cyberama*. After a brief hold, they speak to the cybercrime division of the FBI and explain the situation. They then call the coordinators of Project X.

I turn to Dave and say, "Thank you, Dave. Thanks for being with me through this!"

"Anytime, Maya! So, tomorrow same time, same place to play Level 7 of *Cyberama*," he asks jokingly.

"Noooooo, no more cyber mania!" I say, laughing aloud.

15

THE END—OR THE BEGINNING?

The next day, a few officers from the FBI visit our house. One of them introduces themselves as coming from the cybercrime division, with specialization in **cyber forensics**. He explains that he'll be examining our tablets for any digital evidence that could lead to identifying the location of the criminals who created *Cyberama*. The officers interview me, Dave, and my cyber pals for a few hours. We explain all that happened in detail and give them the address of the building on Hartsdale Avenue. An officer dispatches his fellow mate to the address, then makes a phone call. Forty-five minutes later, two computer programmers arrive at our house. Dave and I hand over our tablets for investigation. Cyber Panda explains how he couldn't trace the location of the criminals from their IP address. The programmers install the *Cyberama* game back on my tablet and spend a few hours decoding the game. They connect my tablet to theirs and start typing fast.

My head starts spinning looking at constantly scrolling pages of letters and numbers that look like complex computer code. Dave and I take the next two days off from school as the investigation continues. On the third day, around three o' clock in the afternoon, one of the computer programmers gasps, raises his hands, and smiles in victory, saying, "YES!" The officers move towards him, look at his computer, and congratulate him. They then thank Dave's family and mine for our cooperation and leave our house.

A week later, my parents tell me that the cyber-criminals were actually spies from the neighboring government, who created this game specifically for Dave and me in order to steal information about Project X through my tablet. It looks like they found out about me from an internet search with my unique name, "Maya Saanvi Iyer." They targeted Dave after another internet search revealed that he and I go to the same school. Dave's name also appeared on his chess club roster, which was published on the internet for everyone to see. The criminals had rented out an entire building to run clandestine operations under the name of a video-game company. Thanks to my cyber pals, Dave and I were able to save the day.

Dave and I still meet regularly and play online games. We now know what kind of information to provide on the internet, and how to be cautious when ads or pop-ups show up.

So yeah, that's how this twelve-year-old American Indian New Yorker, Maya Iyer, who feels lost most of the time and is still trying to figure out who she really is, went to different places, along with crazy, wacky, cyber-y bots, and fought dangerous cybercriminals!

● ● ●

A year later, my parents received an invitation from the White House to accept an award from the President of the United States for their research for

Project RemediX. The project was being referred to as Project X by their team all along. The medicine my parents invented as part of the project would go on to save millions of lives! The spies from the neighboring government were trying to steal the formula of the medicine and use it for the good of their own country, instead of sharing it with the rest of the world. And then, the most surprising thing happened! My parents mentioned that they could bring one accompanying guest to watch them accept the award. Guess who that special guest was? Yours truly! My happiness knew no bounds, and I was super excited to visit the White House! I earned this one, you see!

A month later, we traveled to Washington D.C. to visit the White House. My parents and I visited the White House a few years ago as tourists, but this was our first time inside! I stared at the magnificent building. Behind the green shrubs were lots of trees, beautiful gardens, fountains, and tons of security. The building with its tall white pillars stood glorious in front of us!

As I entered the White House, my jaw dropped looking at the shiny floors, large chandeliers, and tall

ceiling. It felt as if we were entering a grand ballroom. After passing the security check, my parents and I were accompanied by a few officials to the award ceremony.

We entered a small room that had the United States flag and large paintings of past presidents in golden frames. There were about fifteen people inside the room, and we were seated in cushiony chairs with dark blue velvet fabric. A few minutes later, everyone rose from their seats as the President walked in. I stood there, staring at the President without blinking, for two minutes straight! After congratulating the team of Project RemediX, the President shook hands, one by one, until she got to my parents. I couldn't hear what they were talking about, but the President turned her head towards me and winked! The President of the United States of America winked at me, y'all! I couldn't wait to tell my class. They might not believe me, but I knew Dave would. It was officially the best day in my life, EVER!

My parents thanked me again for protecting the formula of the medicine. We flew back that evening to New York. My parents and I stopped for some frozen

yogurt on the way back. I picked my usual favorite—a mix of birthday cake and cookie dough, with sprinkles and just the right amount of marshmallows on top. We walked into the sunset for what seemed like a peaceful evening.

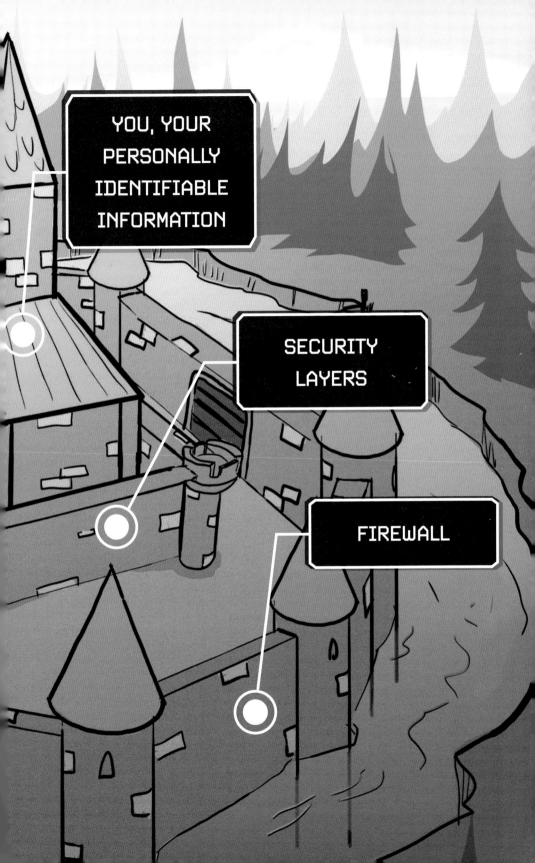

GLOSSARY

Artificial Intelligence or AI – Computers made to think and act like people.

Bad actor – General term for a bad person; for example, a cybercriminal hacker with bad intentions, who attempts to steal others' personal information online.

Bot – Robots that are made to look and act like people or animals.

Bootloader mode – The first few things that computers check for before they are ready for use.

Cyberbully – A person who bullies online using cell phones, emails, computer games or social media.

Cybercriminal – A person with bad intentions who steals others' information online to make money or to commit crimes.

Digital – Information that we see or that is stored in a computer or a device.

Digital evil twin – A twin version of someone that is created online to do harm.

Doxing or doxxing – Based on the word "document"; sharing someone's personal information online without their permission.

Firewall – A way of protecting information on a computer by creating a secure fence (like a wall of fire).

Hacker – A person with good or bad intentions who gains access to others' computers.

> **Types of hackers:**
>
> **White Hat Hacker (good)** – A hacker who finds and blocks online attacks on computers.
>
> **Gray Hat Hacker (good or bad)** – A hacker who gains access to others' computers, but not necessarily with bad intentions.
>
> **Black Hat Hacker (bad)** – A hacker who gains access to others' computers to do harm.
>
> **Blue Hat Hacker (good or bad)** – A hacker who helps companies test software for security or launches attacks on computers.
>
> **Green Hat Hacker (bad)** – A kid or a young adult doing harm online while still learning computers, also called a "script kiddie".
>
> **Red Hat Hacker (good)** – Similar to white hat hacker. One who finds and fights online attacks on computers.

Hardware – A physical device like computer, tablet or online gaming console.

Identity Theft – Stealing someone's information to do harm or to make money.

IP address – Electronic address of a computer connected to a network.

Malware – Common term for computer software that is created to do harm.

> **Types of malware:**
>
> **Adware** – Harmful computer programs that are displayed as ads or free offers.
>
> **Ransomware** – Harmful computer programs that block our computers until we pay money.
>
> **Spyware** – Harmful computer programs that spy on our online activities without our knowledge.

Virus – Most common of the harmful computer programs that damage or delete information.

Worm – Harmful computer program that multiplies itself and spreads to other computers.

Metaverse – A virtual world or a fictional universe with digital characters that interact with real people.

Modem – A device that helps you connect to the internet.

Network – A group of connected computers that share information.

Types of networks:

Secured Network – A safe, password protected network.

Unsecured Network – An unprotected network, easy for a bad actor to attack.

Pharming – A phishing attack where a hacker installs harmful software to a computer to send someone to fake websites.

Phishing – An online attack where a bad actor sends real looking email with harmful links.

PII – Personally Identifiable Information – example's inlcude name, birthdate, address, car license number, credit card number or school ID number.

Smishing – A phishing attack based on SMS (Short Message/Messaging Service) or text.

Social Engineering – Tricking someone into providing personal information. *See PII*

Software – Computer programs that make devices work.

Supercomputer – A powerful computer that can perform much faster than an ordinary computer.

Virtual Reality – Using computer programs to make people and objects that look real.

Vishing – A phishing attack based on voicemail or phone.

Whale phishing – A phishing attack specifically created to target rich people, also called big fish.

ABOUT THE AUTHOR

Arthi Vasudevan is a senior cybersecurity product manager with fifteen years of experience in engineering and cybersecurity. She is also a mom of two young children who have recently started using the internet. Originally from India, she currently lives in Texas. She is passionate about promoting STEM and cyber safety in young children through interactive workshops and games. She also speaks at various industry conferences, and has organized multiple events on career development for professionals.

ABOUT THE ILLUSTRATOR

Jasmin Davis is a talented digital artist. She has been creating artwork since childhood including digital painting, illustration, character and lighting design, concept art, and traditional art. As an artist, she loves exploring all styles and mediums, but her style of drawing is classified as "stylized semi-realism." Her recent interest has been to study artwork around cinematic photography.

Visit www.cyberama.org for resources, games, and more!